SEXUAL ABUSE BY CLERGY:
A Crisis for the Church

MARIE M. FORTUNE
Executive Director
The Center for the Prevention of Sexual & Domestic Violence
Seattle, Washington, U.S.A.

JAMES N. POLING
Professor of Pastoral Theology and Counseling
Colgate Rochester/Bexley Hall/Crozer Theological Seminary
Rochester, New York, U.S.A.

With an Introduction by
LARRY KENT GRAHAM
Professor of Pastoral Theology and Care
Iliff School of Theology
Denver, Colorado, U.S.A.

JPCP Monograph No. 6

©Journal of Pastoral Care Publications, Inc.
1549 Clairmont Rd., Suite 103
Decatur, GA 30033-4611

1994

CONTENTS

SEXUAL ABUSE BY CLERGY:
A Crisis for the Church

©Journal of Pastoral Care Publications, Inc.
ISBN 0-929670-09-4

INTRODUCTION

Larry Kent Graham

lergy sexual abuse is a horrible reality. These essays reveal that between ten and twenty percent of clergy offend against the integrity of the pastoral relationship and the vulnerability of those entrusted to their care by crossing the boundary from religious service to sexual activity. The survivors of such abuse face terrible consequences of personal and relational brokenness and the loss of God and the church. The church and pastoral care and counseling agencies become conflicted by competing claims about responsibility and paralyzed by the threat of costly lawsuits from all involved parties. And the ongoing failure to bring perpetrators to account and to bring about vindication for the survivors undermines the vitality of our religious communities, and the credibility of our message.

In these essays, based upon oral presentations given at plenary sessions at the annual convention of the American Association of Pastoral Counselors in Louisville, Kentucky in April of 1993, Marie Fortune and James Poling explore the devastating reality of clergy sexual misconduct. Dr. Marie M. Fortune, a clergywoman in the United Church of Christ, directs the Center for the Prevention of Sexual and Domestic Violence in Seattle, Washington. She has long been an international leader in the field of sexual and domestic violence, and since 1984 her center has responded to nearly 2000 instances of clergy sexual abuse. Her book, *Is Nothing Sacred? When Sex Invades the Pastoral Relationship*, sets the standard for assessing and responding to exploitive clergy sexual misconduct.

Dr. James N. Poling is an ordained clergyman and Professor of Pastoral Theology and Counseling at Colgate-Rochester Divinity School in Rochester, New York. He is a Fellow in the American Association of Pastoral Counselors and past President of the Society of Pastoral Theology. His clinical and theoretical work has been with incest perpetrators. His well-known book, *The Abuse of Power: A Theological Problem*, details the theological and cultural factors accounting for incest, and points to the need for a transformed theology if we are to hold perpetrators accountable and help survivors recover.

Marie has many gifts as a person and as a pastor, but perhaps the greatest is her unwavering clarity about the core ethical issue of clergy sexual abuse. Over and over, she has made it clear that when clergy cross sexual boundaries with parishioners and counselees, they have betrayed the trust placed in them and have failed to fulfill their role as *clergy* persons. No matter what other personal ethical issues may be involved — such as adultery, addiction and burnout — the core issue in clergy misconduct is the violation of clergy professional ethics rather than of personal sexual ethics. From her we have become aware that because of the unequal levels of power between ministers and parishioners, there can be no genuine consent and that any intimacy which might exist is finally pseudo intimacy and ultimately damaging. Further, she has helped us to see that it is not enough for the offending minister to take responsibility for his or her actions, but that the church must also respond if there is to be prevention, justice-making, and ultimate healing for all parties.

It has not always been easy for ministers and pastoral counselors to hear this message. There are many reasons for this, but chief among them is the ethos we have inherited from the sixties and seventies that protested restrictive boundaries and hierarchies of power. Human potential groups abounded in which persons thought that genuine human fulfillment consisted of establishing emotional and sexual intimacy in spite of society's puritanical and oppressive sexual norms. Open marriage was celebrated; authentic human encounter was increasingly the criteria of liberating ministry.

During this period, clergy themselves were trying to break through to new and more authentic forms of personhood, which included a variety of sexual options. The therapy room and pastoral counseling office was seen by some as the place where intimacy, including sexual intimacy, could be safely experienced as a protest against restrictive sexual attitudes and as a foundation for increased humanization of the larger world. The liberation of sexuality and the new doctrines of mutuality, egalitarian power between men and women, and authentic encounter as avant garde ministry, obscured the recognition of the necessity of a real power differential in the minister/

parishioner relationship in order to protect both the vulnerable parishioner and the integrity of the ministry. Obscuring this power differential was another way in which clergy and pastoral counselors perpetuated the male abuse of women in our patriarchal culture.

Marie deserves our gratitude for her persistence in helping us become clear about clergy responsibility, and to hold ourselves accountable so that real healing and justice-making may occur. Her essays in this volume reveal her as a master teacher on these themes, as well as demonstrating her clear insight into the power dynamics which make forgiveness an inappropriate moral requirement of victims. She provides clear-headed assessments of what is required for prevention, justice-making and healing in the face of the resistance and backlashes presently emerging in the church and society.

In Jim Poling the reader will find a love for theological education, process theology, and a passion for justice in gender relationships. One of Jim's greatest contributions is the recognition that all human issues are fundamentally *theological* issues, and that all clinical work requires both theological and social analysis if the liberating potentials inherent in each are to be realized. Jim speaks from his pain as both an inheritor and victim of the patriarchal religious system so dominant in our culture. Yet, his presentations are not "merely" personal autobiography. They are incisive pastoral theological interpretations which move from the concrete, "palpable immediacies" of pain and internalized wounding objects, through disciplined social and theological analysis, to a critical revisiting of the injuring context in light of a transformative theology and practice. It is among the freshest and most liberating pastoral theological thinking that I know about.

The abiding contribution that James Poling makes in these essays is his linking of the particularities of the counseling process to larger cultural and theological currents accounting for clergy abuse. Based upon his analysis of white male patriarchal culture and the Christian salvation stories embodied in this culture, Poling demonstrates that when male clergy abuse female parishioners they are expressing the norms of our Christian cultural heritage rather than representing an aberration of those norms. He convincingly argues that when pastoral caregivers and ministers remain within the horizon of psychodynamic and interpersonal categories, we further the cultural reality of misogynist abuse. To be transformative, pastoral care and counseling must incorporate a social analysis, such as provided by feminist, womanist, and gay and lesbian liberationists, into psychodynamic and theological viewpoints. Jim provides a splendid example of such an analysis and carries us a long way forward if we can hear him.

The core theme of these essays is the need to rethink and reconstitute power, including our view of God's power, into genuinely mutual and accountable arrangements. Healing, intimacy, reconciliation and forgiveness derive from justice and vindication, rather than vice versa. The healing and restoration of persons, and a genuine social advance, will come only when we are able to reconceive power and order our practice of ministry, care and counseling in non-coercive and non-patriarchal terms. The challenge is a cultural challenge, with serious consequences for elevating those of low degree and bringing the mighty down to the possibility of genuine redemption.

To move forward, we need not only the kind of clarity and assessment that these essays provide. We also need a safer and stronger environment. Dr. Christie Cozad Neuger, Professor of Pastoral Care and Counseling at United Seminary of the Twin Cities, was one of the respondents to these plenary presentations. She raised the question to Poling about why he said more about the pain and hope of surviving women than he did about the accountability and recovery of offending male pastors. Poling's answer was instructive. He said something like, "It is too painful to talk about because it is too unsafe. We do not have a safe place for men to face what we have done and what it has cost us and others. Until we can make it more safe we can't be accountable and restored." It would be easy to dismiss these words as self-serving — especially by a powerful white male who is by no means "unsafe" in the same way women and others are unsafe in our churches and culture. Yet, Poling correctly recognizes that the courage to face the pain of accountability and recovery requires a proper milieu. Men have come to be relatively comfortable in the milieu in which coercive power prevails; it would seem that a context which nurtures genuine accountability, self-discovery, and transformation for abusive men is still a horizon away.

CHAPTER 1

WHEN SEX INVADES
THE MINISTERIAL RELATIONSHIP

Marie M. Fortune

The book of Ezekiel, in which God instructs Ezekiel to prophesy to the shepherds of Israel, is a good place to begin a consideration of ministerial misconduct involving sexual abuse of congregants or clients:

> Trouble for the shepherds of Israel who feed themselves! Shepherds ought to feed their flock, yet you have fed on milk, you have dressed yourselves in wool, you have sacrificed the fattest sheep, but failed to feed the flock. You have failed to make the weak sheep strong, or to care for the sick ones, or bandage the wounded ones. You have failed to bring back strays or look for the lost. On the contrary, you have ruled them cruelly and violently ...
>
> Well then, shepherds, hear the word of Yahweh. As I live, I swear it — it is the Lord Yahweh who speaks — since my flock has been looted and for lack of bothering about my flock, since my shepherds feed themselves rather than my flock, in view of all this, shepherds, hear the word of Yahweh. The Lord Yahweh says this: I am going to call the shepherds to account. I am going to take my flock back from them and I shall not allow them to feed my flock. In this way the shepherds will stop feeding themselves. I shall rescue my sheep from their mouths; they will not prey on them any more. (Ezekiel 34:2-5, 7-10, Jerusalem Bible)

In this chapter, I will define and describe the problem of sexual abuse by clergy and pastoral counselors, as well as its consequences, and encourage our responsibility to assist its victims in finding a just response from our religious institutions. In Chapter 2, I will analyze the political context of this discussion, make a case for the importance of clear policy and standards, and discuss the current status of our efforts.

All clergy and ministers have friendships with congregants and clients and have at times experienced sexual attraction to some of them; all clergy and ministers have received sexual "come ons" from congregants and clients; to some extent, all clergy and ministers have violated the boundaries of the ministerial relationship, if not sexually, then emotionally.

These words may seem like powerful indictments against the ministry and ministerial counseling. Yet to deny the truth of these assertions is to lack understanding of them as facts of life. Our professions, unlike many others, bring us into some of the most intimate, sacred and fragile dimensions of others' lives. Paradoxically, it is because of these intimate connections that ministers and ministerial counselors face the risk of engaging in inappropriate or unethical behavior with those whom we serve or supervise.

From the perspective of the institutional church or synagogue which carries responsibility for the professional conduct of its clergy, the task is twofold: to maintain the integrity of the ministerial relationship and in so doing, to protect those who may be vulnerable to clergy, i.e., congregants, clients, staff members, students, etc.

SCOPE OF THE PROBLEM

The minister violates the relationship boundary with a congregant, student or employee by sexualizing that relationship. When this happens in a ministerial or counseling relationship, it is similar to the violation of the therapeutic relationship by a therapist. When the minister sexualizes the supervisory or mentor relationship with a staff member or student, it is similar to sexual harassment in the workplace and the principles of workplace harassment apply. When a child or teenager is the object of the sexual contact, the situation is one of pedophilia or child sexual abuse, which is by definition not only unethical and abusive but criminal.

Sexual contact by ministers and pastoral counselors with congregants/clients undercuts an otherwise effective pastoral relationship and violates the trust necessary in that relationship. It is not the sexual contact per se that is problematic but the fact that the sexual activity takes place within the pastoral relationship. The crossing of this particular boundary is significant because it changes the nature of the relationship and the resulting potential harm is enormous.

Behaviors occurring in the sexual violation of boundaries include, but are not limited to, sexual comments or suggestions (jokes, innuendos, invitations, etc.), touching, fondling, seduction, kissing, intercourse, molestation, rape, etc. There may be only one incident or a series of incidents or an ongoing intimate relationship over a period of time.

Such contact instigated by ministers or ministerial counselors is an instance of professional misconduct that is often minimized or ignored. It is not "just an affair," although it may involve an on-going sexual relationship with a client or congregant. It is not merely adultery, although adultery may be a consequence if the minister/counselor or congregant/ client is in a committed relationship. It is not just a momentary lapse of judgment by the minister or counselor. Often it is a recurring pattern of misuse of the ministerial role by one who seems to neither comprehend nor care about the damaging effects it may have on the recipient.

Actual research on clergy sexual involvement with congregants is sparse. However, a 1984 study provides some data: 12.67% of clergy surveyed reported that they had had sexual intercourse with a church member. This percentage is the same across lines of denomination, theological orientation, and gender. It does not compare favorably with other helping professions, as among clinical psychologists, only 5.5% of males and 0.6% of females reported sexual intercourse with clients.[1] Thus, twice as many clergy self-report sexual intercourse with congregants as do psychologists. In addition, 76.51% of clergy in this study reported knowledge of another minister who had had sexual intercourse with a church member.[2] However, the research which is most needed to give us a clear picture of the extent of this problem is a survey of the laity.

Research on sexual harassment in the church workplace is also limited. In 1985, when the United Church of Christ in the U.S. asked its clergywomen if they had experienced sexual harassment in the church by senior ministers, supervisors, etc., 47% responded affirmatively. A similar study done by the United Methodists in 1990 found 77% of clergy–women experiencing sexual harassment as staff members or students.

Although the vast majority of ministerial offenders in reported cases are heterosexual males and the vast majority of victims are heterosexual females, it is clear that neither gender nor sexual orientation exclude anyone from the roles of possible offenders or victims in the ministerial or counseling relationship.

CONSEQUENCES

The psychological effect on a congregant/client of sexual contact with their minister/counselor is profound. Initially, the client/congregant may feel flattered by the special attention and may even be seen as "consenting" to the activity. Frequently, however, the congregant/client has sought ministerial care during a time of crisis and is very vulnerable. (Commonly, persons who are exploited by a minister or pastoral counselor have some history of childhood sexual abuse which may or may not have been addressed. Being a survivor of child sexual abuse only increases their vulnerability to further exploitation.) Eventually the congregant/client begins to realize that she or he is being denied a much-needed ministerial relationship and begins to feel used. The recipient of this attention feels betrayed, victimized, confused, embarrassed and fearful, ready to accept blame, and, at this point, unlikely to discuss this situation with anyone and so remains isolated. When anger finally surfaces, the individual is then ready to break the silence and take some action on behalf of self and others.

Spiritually the consequences are also profound; the psychological pain is magnified and takes on cosmic proportions. Not only is the congregant/client betrayed by one representing God but also betrayed by God and the church or synagogue. For this person, the minister/counselor is powerful and can easily manipulate a victim, not only psychologically but morally. The result is enormous confusion and guilt: "But he said that love can never be wrong; that God had brought us together"; or, "He said we should sin boldly so that grace might abound." This psychological crisis becomes a crisis of faith, as well, and the stakes are high.

AN ETHICAL ANALYSIS

It is a violation of professional ethics for any person in a ministerial role of leadership or counseling (clergy or lay) to engage in sexual contact or sexualized behavior with a congregant, client, employee, student, etc. of any age, within the professional relationship.

Why is it wrong for a minister to be sexual with someone whom he or she serves or supervises? It is wrong because sexual activity *in this context* is exploitive and abusive.

First, it is a violation of role. The ministerial relationship presupposes certain role expectations. The minister/counselor is expected to make available certain resources, talents, knowledge, and expertise which will serve the best interests of the congregant, client, staff member, student intern, etc. Sexual contact is not part of the ministerial, professional role.

Second, it is a misuse of authority and power. The role of minister/counselor carries with it authority and power and the attendant responsibility to use this power to benefit the people who call upon the minister/counselor for service. This power can easily be misused, as is the case when a professional uses, intentionally or otherwise, his or her authority to initiate or pursue sexual contact with a congregant, client, etc. Even if it is the congregant who sexualizes the relationship, it is still the minister/counselor's responsibility to maintain the boundaries of the ministerial relationship and not pursue a sexual relationship.

Third, it is taking advantage of vulnerability. The congregant, client, employee, student intern, etc. is by definition vulnerable to the minister/counselor, i.e., in multiple ways, she/he has fewer resources and less power than the minister/counselor. When the latter takes advantage of this vulnerability to gain sexual access to her or him, that constitutes a violation of the mandate to protect the vulnerable from harm. The protection of the vulnerable is a practice which derives from the Jewish and Christian traditions of a hospitality code.

Fourth, it is an absence of meaningful consent. Meaningful consent to sexual activity requires a context of choice, but also mutuality and equality; hence meaningful consent requires the absence of fear or the most subtle coercion. There is always an imbalance of power and thus inequality between the person in the ministerial role and those whom the minister/counselor supervises. Even in the relationship between two persons who see themselves as "consenting adults," the difference in role precludes the possibility of meaningful consent.

The summary of an ethical analysis of the sexualization by clergy of a ministerial relationship is the measure of harm caused by the betrayal of trust inherent in each of these four factors. Important boundaries within the ministerial or counseling relationship are crossed and as a result trust is betrayed. The sexual nature of this boundary violation is significant only in that the sexual context is one of great vulnerability and fragility for most people. However, the essential harm is that of betrayal of trust.

Traditional sexual ethics, whether conservative or liberal, have fallen woefully short in addressing the problem of sexual activity between clergy and their congregants, clients, etc. For conservatives, the issue is always framed in terms of adultery, i.e., the minister being involved in sex outside of marriage. This view of the ethical problem misses the point and is analogous to framing a father's incestuous abuse of his child as adultery. While it is certainly the case that a married minister who engages in sexual activity with a congregant is committing adultery, the adultery should be seen as the *consequence* of the primary ethical problem, which is the professional misconduct and violation of ministerial boundaries. Adultery is *an* issue and one which causes great pain for the minister's family; it is secondary, however, to the harm caused by the minister in his or her professional role.

Liberals on the other hand have hesitated to frame the issue at all. In recent years, some denominations have made a well-motivated effort to limit the church's or synagogue's involvement in a clergyperson's personal, sexual life. Here the predominant norms have been "judge not that you not be judged" and "sex is God's gift to be shared with someone you love." Unfortunately one consequence of this stance has been a laissez-faire sexual ethic which has meant that the liberal church has had no *professional* ethic regarding clergy sexual involvement with congregants, clients, etc.

In both case, because the church has approached the reality of clergy sexual involvement with congregants, clients, etc. as a "sexual" issue, it has been devoid of resources with which to adequately address what is in fact an issue of *professional misconduct.*

JUSTICE-MAKING

If we look to our theology as a resource in shaping our response to sexual abuse by a minister or pastoral counselor, we can begin to understand what is required for healing to occur. In scripture we learn about a God who stands with the powerless, who will not let the powerful go unchallenged, who takes sides, who seeks not punishment but repentance for the abuser, who carries the victim through the valley of the shadow. All of these are aspects of justice-making.

The other source of our learning about how to respond to harm done to another is to listen to victims and survivors. If we ask them, they will tell us what they need to find healing. These are the things they say:

> "I want to tell him what this has done to me."
> "I want him to acknowledge what he did and take responsibility for it."
> "I want to make sure that he can't do this to anyone else."
> "I want her to pay for my therapy expenses."
> "I want his name removed from the building at the seminary."

These are reasonable, concrete actions which carry a tremendous meaning for victims and survivors. They are acts of justice which we as administrators, therapists, advocates, and ministers can help to bring about.

These actions can promote justice-making, which includes these aspects:

— truth-telling: an opportunity for the survivor to tell her/his story
— acknowledgement: confirmation by the institution that the survivor has been heard and believed and that what occurred was wrong
— compassion: a willingness to suffer with the survivor and not merely to problem-solve
— protection of the vulnerable: taking any necessary steps to prevent harm to anyone else

— accountability for the abuser: calling the abuser to account so that repentance and healing may be possible
— restitution: material payment to the survivor to cover therapy and medical expenses, etc.
— vindication: freedom from the burden of the memories and scars caused by the victimization.[3]

Usually not all of these aspects of justice-making are possible, but once some aspects of justice have been fulfilled, healing can begin. Only then is it possible to even begin to talk about forgiveness.

THE PROBLEM WITH FORGIVENESS

The biggest problem with forgiveness is that most people seem to see it as the first step rather than the last. They also seem to mean by "forgiveness" that an abuser should not be held accountable. When there is some indication that harm has been done, the first response for many people is "the Bible says we should forgive and forget." This is best translated as: "We (those who have responsibility as leaders) don't want to know about this and we don't want to have to do anything about it, so can't we just pretend it never happened?" No one is served by this response: certainly not the victim/survivor, but also not the perpetrator. This is cheap grace and it never leads to repentance and healing for anyone.

Invited to attend an incest offenders group to discuss religious issues, I sat in a circle with 27 offenders, 25 of whom were Christians. When each of them had been arrested for sexual molestation, they went immediately to their minister. Each of them said he was prayed over and sent home forgiven. As we went around the circle, they all said, "Whenever you talk to clergy, tell them for us: 'Don't forgive us so quickly.'" They made it very clear that this quick forgiveness had only helped them continue to minimize the harm they had caused and avoid responsibility for it.

I have known for a long time that cheap grace does not suffice in the face of victimization. Having listened to victims and survivors, I have seen the further damage done when justice is bypassed to make the powers-that-be more comfortable. I have struggled to comprehend my own dis-ease at the platitudinous advice to forgive and forget.

Some understanding of the scriptural basis for this discomfort has come from an unpublished paper written by Frederick Keene. He examines the Christian scriptural references to forgiveness in light of a power analysis, arguing that interpersonal forgiveness is possible only when the forgiver is more powerful than, or an equal of, the forgiven. "... it is not possible ... for one person to forgive another person of greater power.... The tenant can forgive a financial wrong only of a financial equal (or inferior). A wife can forgive a marital wrong only as a marital equal. Within the Christian context, a landlord might be expected to forgive the debts of his tenants, but he can not and should not expect to be forgiven for any wrongs he has committed — unless, possibly, he ceases to be a landlord."[4]

Keene points out that one of the terms for "forgive" is the word meaning "to dismiss" or "to divorce." Since divorce was a process controlled by the husband, this connotation of forgiveness could only come from the more powerful person. But the most common word for "forgiveness" is a commercial term generally meaning "to forgive a debt." Here we usually find ". . . a more powerful being, whether God or a person, releasing another from a debt or an obligation or a penalty." Thus forgiveness of sins has to do with release from the penalty of sin or debt; it does not refer to cleansing.

Keene observes that Christian scripture generally discusses forgiveness in terms of God or Jesus forgiving sins and the words used almost always have juridical or commercial overtones. Rarely does the text discuss people forgiving each other. The two are connected in this petition in the Lord's prayer: ". . . forgive us our debts as we forgive our debtors." This recognizes a hierarchy and that forgiveness flows down from the most powerful to the least: we ask God, who has ultimate power, to let go of our debts as we commit ourselves to letting go of the debts of those who have less power than we do. In the commercial analogy, the creditor has power over the one who is indebted and is thus in a position to let go of the debt. The reverse is not true. We find no reference to a situation in which we have a grievance against one who has power over us and no expectation that we forgive that more powerful person.

There are however two references to forgiveness between equals in Matthew 18.21-22 and Luke 17.3-4:

> Be on your guard. If another disciple sins, you must
> rebuke the offender, and if there is repentance, you must
> forgive. And if the same person sins against you seven
> times a day, and turns back to you seven times and says
> 'I repent,' you must forgive.

Here, between equals, we find forgiveness tied directly to 1) confronta-
tion of the offender and 2) repentance by the offender. This is the context
of justice-making in which forgiveness by another person is possible if
there is repentance. And repentance means change: "Repent: get a new
heart and a new mind."

Finally, when Jesus hangs from the cross, stripped of his power
and his dignity, he does not forgive those who crucified him. He turns to
God and asks God to forgive them because they don't know what they are
doing. Keene comments: "This is the one place where, if Jesus wanted the
weak to forgive the strong, he could have indicated it. He did not."[5]

What are the implications for our pastoral and institutional practice? Keene argues, and I agree, that there is never a suggestion in
Christian scripture that the less powerful are expected to forgive the more
powerful. For the victim of pastoral abuse, then, the one who came into
the pastoral relationship with fewer resources and who is rendered even
more powerless by the victimization she or he experiences there, forgiveness of her or his abuser is not an option. It can only become an option if
the more powerful person relinquishes power. This is most concretely
accomplished by the payment of restitution, by the relinquishment of
status and role, such as ordination or licensing, by acknowledgment of the
reality of the abuse and responsibility for it. These are acts of repentance
which can empower the victim/survivor, establish justice, then make
forgiveness a possibility.

The making of justice presupposes some fundamental under-
standings of power. First, we must recognize and name the differences in
power that exist among us as a result of various factors, including gender,
race, sexual orientation, age, class, physical ability, life circumstance,
role, etc. A truly peer relationship is unusual, and even then equality may
be only relative. In every relationship, we find ourselves with more or less
power than the other or with relatively .equal power. Some of these
inequalities of power are givens in life: children will always be less
powerful than adults, persons who are ill or disabled have fewer resources

12

than those who are not. In these circumstances, the Hebrew hospitality code always applies: we are expected to protect those who are vulnerable or who have fewer resources to cope with life.

But there are other inequalities in life which, while they are very much with us today, are wrong, such as those resulting from sexism, racism, agism, heterosexism, etc. At the same time that we recognize the existence of these inequalities, we must be working to remove them. This is not to be confused with denying their existence. For example, when white people say they are colorblind in a racist society, they deny the reality that people of color generally have less access to resources than do whites. Denying this fact does not erase it. Instead, for those of us who are white, it is our job to use whatever access our whiteness affords us to open doors and change racist structures, so that people of color can have access. At the same time, we also must use whatever power we have to protect those who are vulnerable. In other words, when we have a degree of power in relation to another, it is our job to use it to help empower the other, to increase that person's access to resources, rather than increase their dependence on us or enable us to take advantage of them. Understanding our own power, its limits and implied responsibility, is fundamental to the practice of ministry or pastoral counseling. Finally, understanding that in the roles of minister or pastoral counselor, we are in a fiduciary relationship with a congregant, client, student, staff member, etc. This means we are emphatically obligated to act in their best interests.

PREVENTION

Finally, a word about prevention. Prevention involves development of clear policy on sexual abuse by clergy or pastoral counselors, education at all levels of the ministry, and support for individual self-care for clergy and lay professionals.

> • *An Ethics Policy* — A denominational or professional organization needs to have a clear, unequivocal policy stating that clergy or lay professional sexual contact with congregants, clients, etc. is unethical and unacceptable. The language needs to provide enough specifics to be clear about the parameters of the professional conduct. (Within most denominational mate-

rials, this kind of misconduct is simply defined as "an act or omission contrary to Scriptures or the Constitution," or "conduct unbecoming the ministry." Lack of specificity allows for confusion and hesitancy to act. One Presbyterian minister who had multiple complaints of professional misconduct involving sexual abuse filed against him said: "Where is it written that I cannot do these things?" It was an effective defense.)

- *Education and Training* — Seminarians and all clergy and pastoral counselors need in-depth training in dealing with boundaries, dual relationships, sexuality, appropriate referrals, stress, etc. They also need mechanisms whereby they can seek regular, qualified consultation and/or supervision in the practice of ministry.

- *Minister/Counselor Self-Care* — All ministers/counselors need to regularly monitor their attention to self-care, both personally and professionally. Guidance from the consultation process can be extremely helpful here.

Prevention can help many ministers and pastoral counselors minimize the risk of crossing boundaries of the ministerial or counseling relationship. It can help prevent their wandering unconsciously across boundaries, which can have devastating consequences. But prevention cannot stop the minister who is a sexual predator; only intervention is effective to remove the predator and prevent others from being harmed.

When prevention fails, we must be ready and willing to use a process of intervention which seeks to bring justice and finally healing to all involved.

CHAPTER 2

DOING SOMETHING ABOUT SEXUAL ABUSE IN THE CHURCH

Marie M. Fortune

ome months ago I spent a long weekend retreat with 33 female survivors of sexual abuse by clergy and pastoral counselors. I listened as they shared their stories about the consequences of sexual abuse in their lives. I heard of undergraduate education cut short, marriages broken, professional careers diverted, and lesbian women seeking help with their confusion about sexual orientation who were only further confused and victimized by the sexual initiatives of their pastors. I heard of mental breakdowns and hospitalization, drug and alcohol abuse, loss of spiritual foundations, and aborted calls to the ministry. These are the stories I hear every day.

When I returned to my office I was confronted with yet another letter from a clergyman who is upset with the work we are doing on clergy ethics and sexual abuse. Lengthy letters like his tell me how misguided we are, how we are blowing all this out of proportion, how women are primarily the offenders in attempts to seduce ministers, how the examples we use in our materials are so extreme as to be unbelievable, and, in particular, how we are really a bunch of hysterical feminists who hate sex and men.

Needless to say, my patience wears thin when I read these letters. My anger, just below the surface all the time, tends to erupt and I wait several weeks before attempting a written response.

While I find these letters aggravating and increasingly resent the time it takes to respond to them, I do understand what they represent. The backlash is alive and well as it actively resists efforts to address violations of professional ethics. As this backlash becomes more organized and vocal, I believe it indicates that those of us who are seeking to change the status quo are making progress. Therefore, I generally see these letters as a sign of hope.

I would like to address two of the areas raised by those who are resistant to dealing with professional ethics among pastoral counselors and ministers.

ANTI-SEXUAL?

First, some have asserted that any effort to provide guidelines or set limits on the sexual activity of a minister or pastoral counselor in his or her professional role is anti-sexual and Puritanical. I must confess that I am still taken aback by this assertion. Why is it that whenever we suggest there are legitimate limits to our sexual activity, i.e., when we take on a professional role of minister or therapist, there are those who cry foul? This position is not unlike that of the overzealous advocate of free speech who believes it is his or her right to yell fire in a crowded theater. We are asserting that for the pastoral counselor or minister, some people are sexually off limits. In suggesting limits to one's professional activities, such as a prohibition against sexual contact with clients or congregants, we are challenging the prerogative of sexual access, which is the heritage of patriarchal institutions and a privilege assumed by a significant number of male, and some female, practitioners. So we should not be surprised that there is a reaction to this challenge.

The other problem with the analysis that setting limits on the sexual conduct of ministers or pastoral counselors is anti-sexual is that it makes an erroneous assumption that the issue is sex. It is not. The issue is power and its misuse by the professional in ways which do not serve the best interests of the client or congregant. The use of the professional's power and authority to initiate sexual contact, thereby crossing this boundary with a client or congregant, or the abdication of the responsibility to set clear boundaries even in the face of sexual initiatives from a client or congregant, are at the heart of the question of professional ethics.

There are a variety of ways in which a professional can cross appropriate boundaries; sexual contact is only one. But it is a serious issue because sexual intimacy is an area of primary significance for most people. The limit on sexual contact with clients or congregants is also behaviorally specific: a code of ethics can say it is unethical to be sexual with a client, congregant, student, etc. just as it can say it is unethical to embezzle funds or breach confidentiality. These behavioral standards can be understood and enforced.

MORAL AGENCY

The second issue raised by the backlash is the assertion that to suggest that a congregant or client who experiences sexual contact with her or his therapist or minister is a "victim" is to deny her or his moral agency. In other words, who are we to say that a client or congregant might not be a fully consenting adult who freely chooses to engage in sex with her or his therapist or minister?

Moral agency is predicated on the possession of power and resources. In other words, to be a moral agent, able to make moral choices and act on them, one must have resources, knowledge, awareness, options, sound judgment, etc. Anything which denies or compromises these resources undercuts moral agency. So, for example, if a client trusts her therapist to know what is best for her, and if that therapist tells her that in order to deal with her marital problems, she should have sex with him, she is likely to submit willingly to his directive. He has power and authority in his role which she respects and which then undercuts her own best judgment. Likewise, when a minister tells a congregant that God has brought them together, that their "love" could never be wrong, that he would never suggest that they do something wrong, and that to truly know God, the congregant should explore sexual intimacy with the minister, the congregant's sense of morality is compromised. Sexual behavior is being justified by one who serves as a moral guide, and the power and authority of that ministerial role overrides the congregant's best judgment. Under these circumstances moral agency on the part of the client or congregant is compromised. The difference in power between the client/congregant and the therapist/minister precludes authentic consent, which presupposes equality of power in the relationship.

This power differential is not easily rectified. It may be possible for two persons in a pastoral relationship, in which there has been no pastoral counseling and only a relatively superficial relationship, to decide to abandon the pastoral relationship and pursue one on a peer level. However, it is impossible to do so where there has been a therapeutic or counseling relationship.

Our efforts to support congregants and clients who have been misused by ministers or pastoral counselors are labelled as "making victims out of these people," and denying their moral agency. It is ironic, however, that when survivors of abuse and exploitation by ministers or therapists do finally come forward and, acting as moral agents, assert their right not to be exploited, they are castigated as "playing the victim." In fact, they are reclaiming their power and resources and acting in their own best interests to say that the trust they had placed in a minister or therapist was betrayed. Yet when they challenge the power of the professional, they are often ignored or punished for it. Moral agency, which challenges the prerogatives of patriarchal privilege, finds little support in some quarters of the institution.

Finally, in this whole discussion about moral agency, why is there never any mention of it in regard to the professional? This is the person who has the power, resources and subsequent responsibility to protect the vulnerability of the client or congregant. This is the person who holds a fiduciary duty to act always in the best interests of the client or congregant, even when such action is not in the professional's personal interests. It seems to me that the discussion of moral agency should begin here with the professional.

There is no question that increasing the awareness of congregants and clients about appropriate expectations of the minister or therapist, discussing professional ethics openly and de-emphasizing the unquestioned authority of the professional, etc., would prepare consumers to be critical and aware. This would go a long way to prevent their being taken advantage of by unethical professionals and to support their ability to act as moral agents on their own behalf.

ACCOUNTABILITY

The issue which seems to be readily avoided by the backlash is the question of accountability by pastoral abusers. In fact, accountability is the most difficult issue for institutions to face. Many institutional bodies are more interested in protecting predators from the consequences of their behavior than in protecting the people served from predators. Sadly in the final analysis, the institution is not well served by this response. Its credibility is shaken and its liability increased.

A PROGRESS REPORT

Since 1983, the Center for the Prevention of Sexual and Domestic Violence has been addressing the issue of professional ethics and sexual abuse by clergy. That was the year we received our first call for help from a survivor of clergy sexual abuse. Between 1983 and 1993, we have had some contact with well over 1150 cases in the U.S. and Canada. We have served as advocate, minister, or consultant with victims, survivors, offenders, judicatory and seminary administrators, and lawyers.

In 1986, the first U.S. conference on abuse in helping relationships was held in Minneapolis. There we shared questions and strategies across professional disciplines. The title of the conference was significant: "It's Never O.K." By the end of the conference, we wanted to add a subtitle: "And It's Always Our Responsibility." This is the bottom line — *and* it's never simple.

In 1989, *Is Nothing Sacred? When Sex Invades the Ministerial Relationship* was published.[6] This book was the first critical appraisal of the violation of the ministerial relationship which it called an issue of professional ethics and sexual abuse.

The discussion of the problem was expanded; disclosures by victims/survivors have increased; lawsuits against churches, denominations, and pastoral counselors have multiplied. A can of worms has been opened which now challenges our professional credibility and our religious institutions. A number of denominations at the national and regional levels, moving to develop policy and procedures, are being faced with an increasing number of complaints. More research projects are underway and codes of ethics have been written or revised by professional organizations. In theological seminaries, some attention is beginning to be focused on preparing ministers and pastoral counselors to lessen their risk of violating the integrity of the ministerial relationship. As the body of literature increases training and video resources are available from a number of sources.

The good news is that *some* denominational leaders and seminary officials are moving swiftly and carefully to name the problem and to remove offending ministers and counselors in order to protect our institutions from further erosion of credibility. They also are moving effectively to bring healing to victims, survivors, and congregations. The leadership being provided is significant and substantial. Careful, thoughtful, committed leadership is beginning to build a firm foundation for our religious institutions to fulfill their responsibilities. It is clear that education and preparation have empowered them, but they remain few in number and they run the risk of being marginalized for their actions.

However, in many quarters the resistance is strong to policies which state clear standards of professional conduct and to procedures which intervene to stop unprofessional conduct.

All of our efforts are played out against a backdrop of the disclosure and adjudication of one case after another, often involving high profile religious leaders. For example, in the past two years:

> John Howard Yoder's ministerial credentials have been suspended following complaints brought by eight women alleging improper sexual behavior and unsuitable use of overt sexual language. Yoder has accepted the church's action and recommendation that he seek therapy. He is a theologian and ethicist and member of the faculty at the University of Notre Dame.

> John Finch, a Christian psychologist who founded the School of Psychology at Fuller Theological Seminary in Pasadena, lost his license to practice psychology in Washington State after the state examining board found that he had engaged in "repeated acts of immorality and misconduct" with his clients over a span of twenty years. Fuller Seminary had named a building and lectureship after Finch and his portrait was prominently displayed there. After the state psychology board's action, the seminary undertook an internal investigation which resulted in severing all ties with Finch.

> Notre Dame Provost James Tunstead Burtchaell, a Holy Cross Father and prominent theologian, resigned his tenured position after an investigation into charges of sexual contact with male students whom he was counseling.

> Most recently, Archbishop Sanchez of New Mexico resigned, facing charges of his ineffectual handling of pedophile priests in the diocese AND of

his own sexual abuse of young women during the past twenty years.

Although these cases, and hundreds more like them, are a painful reminder of the betrayal of trust by our leaders and of the unfinished business of rectifying these situations, they are also a witness to the fact that the church, synagogue, and academy are beginning to deal with the problem of professional misconduct. Although every case brings us pain and confusion, every case also brings an opportunity to make justice as a means to healing the brokenness.

But even in the efforts to address complaints, results are mixed. Some judicatory and academic administrators, although now informed and prepared with policy and procedures, are still not acting to stop offending ministers or pastoral counselors.

In these situations, it would appear that the agenda which prevails is that it is the institution's mission to

— protect the perpetrator from the consequences of his/her behavior
— keep the abusive behavior a secret
— preserve the facade of pleasantry and normalcy in the institution

The best example of this agenda occurs in cases where a victim of clergy professional misconduct or academic sexual harassment finally sues the church, synagogue or university for damages. Frequently the institution, at the urging of its lawyers, has sought to settle out of court for significant sums of money IF the victim(s) agrees to silence. This institution is more interested in secrecy than justice and is willing to pay people off in order to preserve its public image.

The effect of this doctrine and practice is never healing but rather *de-evangelization:* people are leaving or being driven out of the congregation or seminary because of the professional misconduct of *some* of our clergy, teachers, and pastoral counselors and subsequent lack of response to their complaints. For these people, trust in religious leadership is forever shattered. The credibility of these institutions is on the line.

Why is there so little action in some quarters? Why does it seem to be so difficult for judicatories or professional organizations to act swiftly and unequivocally on behalf of those harmed by offending ministers or pastoral counselors?

I used to think the primary reason for a lack of action was ignorance: leaders lacked information, analysis, and tools with which to act. I assumed, therefore, that education and training would provide what was lacking, after which these leaders, girded with truth and righteousness, would walk into the breach, name and confront the violations of professional ethics which they encountered, and remove offending ministers and pastoral counselors from positions of trust.

My assumption that, when prepared, leaders would be eager to act, has not been borne out. In fact, some judicatory administrators who know better continue to circumvent the process or are stymied when an offending minister or teacher flatly denies charges against him, even in the face of multiple complaints. I have concluded that the primary reason for these occurrences is that for some, there is little will and less courage.

The lack of will has to do primarily with an unwillingness to challenge the privilege of sexual access to congregants, staff, and students which seems all too commonplace within a patriarchal institution.

The lack of courage has emerged in the face of legal anxieties: e.g., offending ministers may threaten to sue the church for slander, libel, or the loss of livelihood. These threats have in many cases halted disciplinary proceedings. Yet an offending minister has no basis on which to win such a suit and has not yet succeeded in doing so.

Ironically, it is another legal threat which may eventually embolden these institutions to act. In lieu of any effective action from their church, synagogue or denomination, many victims/survivors are turning to the courts for redress. People do not want to sue these institutions, but they will if they find themselves not only mistreated but stonewalled in their attempts to find justice.

Legally, the cost is high. The Roman Catholic Church in the U.S. expects to spend $1 billion by the year 2000 in settlements for cases of professional misconduct by clergy.[7] Recent U.S. case law is unequivocal: the institution is responsible for the hiring and supervision of its personnel. If we credential our representatives, we must also be accountable for their actions.

But there are signs of hope and possibility. In a law suit against the local congregation of a nondenominational church for sexual abuse by one of its staff members, a jury found in favor of the survivor and against the church. In a second case involving another survivor and the same perpetrator, the church's lawyers urged the church not to settle but to go back to court. The church council recommended this strategy to the congregation but the congregation overrode the decision and said it now understood that because its minister had harmed several members, congregants should pay for the resulting counseling and expenses. They did the right thing and ironically, it probably cost them less than if they had gone back to court and lost again.

In Donald C. Clark, Jr.'s excellent article in *Christian Century*, he describes the move toward legal intervention in cases of professional misconduct by ministers. He also summarizes the legal system's response and asserts that, "The law is filling a void, a vacuum of leadership caused by the religious community's failure to act promptly and adequately. ... the law is doing what it historically does best: empower the powerless."[8] He also rightly cautions the religious community not to allow its response to be directed by the lawyers. He says, "Justice must be the church's goal. But mimicking or accepting the legal definition of justice will not suffice." He is correct. We cannot abdicate our responsibility by passing this task on to lawyers. We must pursue our agenda of justice-making; the lawyers' job is to assist us with this agenda.

I recently talked with a lawyer with whom I was consulting, who is chair of the Permanent Judiciary Commission in his Presbytery. He launched into a ten-minute tirade about how he sees his church bending over backwards to protect predators who are pastors at the same time that the Presbyterians are going to extremes to prevent the ministry of Rev. Jane Spahr, an ordained Presbyterian minister called to pastor in Rochester, NY, who happens to be a lesbian. Without hesitation he pointed to the hypocrisy of this situation, which exists in every denomination that denies the ministries of gays and lesbians.

We presently see the same scenario in the U.S. military. After the Tailhook incident, which disclosed serious sexual harassment by a number of officers, how can military leaders shamelessly argue that the presence of gays and lesbians threatens the order and morale of the military? Sixty-four percent of the women in the military report sexual abuse by men; it would appear that the greater threat to order and morale is coming from heterosexual males.

The issue, indeed, is sexual abuse and harassment, regardless of one's sexual orientation. This is the message which both the military and religious institutions need to learn.

Development and consistent implementation of prevention and intervention strategies are fundamental steps toward maintaining the integrity of ministerial or teaching relationships. In short, the church, synagogue, or denomination has the right and responsibility to remove ministers or pastoral counselors who are a danger to the well-being of members or clients and the institution as a whole. The cost for *NOT* acting is enormous — morally, spiritually, and legally.

But ultimately William White, author of *Incest in the Organization*, is correct when he observes that establishing policy and procedures is not going to solve this problem. It provides the mechanism, yes; but the commitment must be to a much broader and deeper change in our religious institutions.[9] It will require a commitment to challenge the patriarchal core of our collective religious life.

The only way to mount an effective response to past abuse and the possibility of preventing future abuse by those entrusted with responsibility within our religious communities is if the leaders of our religious institutions will lead. Now is the time for courageous, un-equivocal leadership.

The progress which we report here is primarily the result of the courage of survivors who have come forward and told their stories. They, far more than judicatory administrators, committee members, or work-shop leaders, have broken the silence which has allowed clergy and other ministers to misuse their religious offices for years. It is survivors who have dared to speak the truth of their experiences even, as Audre Lorde has said, "at the risk of having it bruised or misunderstood."

Those persons who have survived abuse by clergy and other ministers and have come forward to break the silence have blessed the Church and Synagogue with the gift of truth-telling and deserve our gratitude. They have called us back to our mission: to name and confront the powers of evil within and among us, to work for justice, healing and wholeness of life.

CHAPTER 3

SEXUAL ABUSE AS
A THEOLOGICAL PROBLEM

James N. Poling

bout ten years ago I began to hear stories I could hardly believe — stories from my students — about sexual abuse by pastors and pastoral counselors, often in addition to the trauma of family abuse. Then, women colleagues at seminaries and in pastoral counseling told me of stories they were hearing and of their own experiences. Then I realized that three of my mentors have abused women in their pastoral counseling ministries. All three were important spiritual and professional supervisors and teachers, and only one has been brought to justice. Facing my own hurt and disappointment, as well as acknowledging the consequences of my distorted training from these men, has been an agonizing struggle.

Finding the stories, the images, the words, the ideas to express my hurt, my sadness, my rage and my fear has been one of the most difficult things in my life. I have begun to feel the fear and hurt of women and men I am close to, including women in my own family. I am so enraged at the arrogance and destructiveness of the abusers, and at the silence and collusion of the church. Sometimes I wonder if I can contain my emotion enough to speak and write on these issues. But I do because of the injustice I see; and because the whole church is in danger if this issue is not addressed.

The pastoral counseling movement has a chance to make a difference. We can help the church to change if we use the skills, insights, and institutional power that we have for justice.

My method in this article is a little bit like pastoral counseling itself. I focus on three types of discourse. First, survivors of sexual abuse, especially their religious experience. Second, feminist and African American womanist theologians and their protest of androcentric theology. Third, my own religious imagination. Out of this mix comes a series of images, figures, plots, and free-associations. My method is like dream interpretation, trying to enter into the world of persons and religious communities and feel the force of what is happening. I believe religion actually works this way. My basic questions are these: *What happens when religious images function in an abusive way? What internal world do these images create? To what extent are these abusive images embedded in the religious symbols themselves?*

The co-author of this monograph, Marie Fortune, has done more than any other person to bring the stories of survivors of clergy sexual abuse to the attention of religious communities.[10] She has been listening to women in workshops and conferences; and religious leaders need to understand what she is hearing. Clergy sexual abuse is not just an issue of confused sexuality, though that would be serious enough. Religious communities are confused about the sexist ways in which women are defined and controlled and about the way male clergy abuse their power in relation to women and children. I have been captured by her analysis and want to understand it further because I have my own questions about how human beings, both male and female, are defined, and about how those who are powerful use images of God to justify and perpetuate their control and abuse.

As pastoral theologians, it is our vocation to understand how the stories, teachings, and practices of our religious institutions affect persons. We need to know how religion functions at the level of the unconscious formation of perceptions and behaviors; that is, how the symbols, ideas, and rituals about God oppress or liberate the human spirit. If the ideas and practices of religious communities are damaging our clients and their families, then we have a responsibility to bring these realities before religious leaders for reexamination. If certain ideas and practices liberate persons, leading to healing and transformation, and bringing about a more just society for everyone, then we need to bring that feedback to our religious communities.

For example, in our pastoral counseling, if certain forms of theology increase the suffering of women and children[11] by refusing to address issues of rape and sexual violence, then we must be prophetic voices to protest such a theology. In fact, I believe this is what we are called to do. Clergy sexual abuse is a form of violence against women and children that is practiced by ten to twenty percent of ordained clergymen,[12] and the silence of the Christian church increases the danger and blocks resources for the healing processes of recovery. Some of us in pastoral counseling are women whose lives and ministries are hindered by discrimination and abuse and can understand the survivors of sexual abuse from our own experience. Most of us in pastoral counseling are men who have various experiences as abused and abusers and we have a ministerial responsibility to serve persons rather than exploit them. All of us in ministry are guides for persons in the healing process and are called to serve the best interests of our clients, parishioners, and students. Whether we are women or men, we are called to solidarity with the vulnerable whose voices have been silenced.

Chuck Gerkin reminded us that the early students in pastoral care and counseling were scandalized by the inability of many religious communities to care for the sick, the mentally ill, and those in prison and poverty. He says:

> Those of us who were attracted to pastoral care in those days were convinced … that in significant ways North American culture had hardened its heart against the cries of those who were oppressed by the conformities that culture demanded.[13]

Listening to those who were excluded from the care of our religious communities is a prophetic vocation. Because of our movement, the attitude toward some of these populations has dramatically changed. Religious communities less frequently blame those who are sick for some moral failing, and more often respond with care and support during the crisis of serious illness. We are part of a prophetic movement that has changed religious communities before, and we must do the same today.

In this chapter I will explore how theology contributes to the existence of clergy sexual abuse, and how it contributes to the silence in religious communities.[14] Since research on survivors of clergy sexual abuse has only begun, I will focus on the research that has come out of reflection with survivors of other forms of sexual abuse. In looking at this research, I am searching for the questions we must ask in order to hear the suffering in these stories. The stories of survivors correspond to the spirited debate within womanist and feminist theology in recent years. I will then look at Christology as an issue that unmasks the assumptions that make clergy sexual abuse possible. Finally, I will ask if there are images of God and humanity which are potentially more healing and transforming of the human spirit.

In my view, clergy sexual abuse is a moral contradiction in religious communities that proclaim God's love and justice for all persons. I believe that we each have responsibility to plumb the depths of our own religious traditions to find the roots of this evil. I will look at a particular form of Protestant pietism and theology, aware that my analysis does not apply to some other Christian traditions, nor to Jewish, Islamic, and other religious traditions. But I hope that my critical reflections will be helpful for all of us in understanding our clients, and will encourage similar efforts with other traditions.

CHRISTIANITY AND INCEST

Annie Imbens, a pastoral theologian, and Ineke Jonker, a feminist historian, both from The Netherlands, report on the experiences of ten women survivors of incest. This heuristic study was designed to see how their religious experience helped or hindered them in coping with abuse. All the survivors reported that the impact of their religious upbringing was primarily negative. The authors suggest that these survivors were able "to put into words the humiliation and denial of all women in Christian churches. The plea of women to put an end to sexism within and outside the church, is reinforced by the words of Christian incest survivors."[15]

What are survivors of sexual abuse saying about Christian theology? I will summarize three areas: a) images of women in the Bible and tradition; b) images of God; c) images of Christian faith and practice.

Images of Women. Without exception, the survivors, as adults, rejected the negative images of Biblical women they had been taught as children. On the one hand, they were supposed to be pure, innocent, and subservient, like Mary, the mother of Jesus. On the other hand, they were labeled seductive, sinful and evil, like Eve who tempted Adam and introduced sin into the world. "I knew I should be stoned," said one survivor.[16] Listen to Nell's story:

"The 'Our Father' says 'Thy will be done.' That made me feel even more guilty....When [my father] did what he liked with me and then I had to sit next to him at the table, he would elbow me conspicuously at the moment that he said, 'Forgive us our trespasses.' As if he wanted to say, 'You see? I'm praying specially for you.' ...Sometimes I asked my father why he kept making me do this. Then he said, 'All women are the same as that first women, Eve. You tempt me. In your heart, this is what you want, just like Eve.' I used to pray, 'God, let is stop.' But God didn't intervene, so I thought, either it really was God's will, or I really was as bad as they said, and this was my punishment."[17]

Images of God. Most survivors identified God with the abuser. "God the Father has such almighty power that it's frightening. My father and God were a lot alike."[18] Listen to another woman:

"God is the Father in heaven who does everything for His children because He loves them. That's what some people say. Well, I'm going to tell God exactly what I think of Him.... God gave me a father who raped and abused me for 30 years.... God gave my little girl a father who wanted to rape her when she was three and a half.... Well thank you very much, God, that you wanted to give me all of this and that you loved me very much. But God, I need nothing more from you, do you hear me? I want absolutely nothing from you; just leave me alone.... Goddammit, let me decide for myself what I want and stop trying to push your way into my life all the time."[19]

Images of Faith and Practice. Given the negative and conflicting images of women and their responsibility to an all-loving Father-God, religion meant that men are closer to God than women, that the proper relationship of women to men is subservience, and that the traditional values of submission and obedience are the essence of Christian faith.

"You must love your neighbor. Not much attention was paid to standing up for yourself (Ellen). You must always be the first to forgive, and you must do so seventy times seventy times (Judith). You must always serve, serve God. Sexuality before and outside of marriage is bad (Margaret). Faith and standing up for yourself are conflicting concepts (Theresa). You must sacrifice your own needs and wants, you mustn't resist, mustn't stand up for yourself, must serve God, mustn't be your own person with your own ego (Amy)."[20]

In anticipation of resistance to their negative conclusions, Imbens and Jonker suggest that when women describe their experiences with God as oppressive, pastors typically say, "But what you're describing isn't God! That is a false god. That is what some people have made of God."[21] The authors caution that this defensive response only reinforces the silencing of many women in the church.

These stories provide a window into the world of persons who have been abused by family members and by the clergy. The importance of these particular witnesses is that their experience corresponds to a debate within womanist and feminist theology in recent years; namely, whether God the Creator can be understood in any way other than Father, and whether Jesus the Son can be redemptive for women.

Jacquelyn Grant, an African American womanist theologian, summarizes this discussion by describing four different approaches to Christology. First, some argue that Jesus himself was not patriarchal and that he modeled equality among his followers, both men and women. A second group argues that while the structure of the Bible is patriarchal, there are themes in Jesus' life and ministry that can provide inspiration for the resistance movements of women and other groups to patriarchal domination. Jesus is not to be emulated in every way but he was a model-breaker who understood human liberation. A third group argues that Christianity is so patriarchal, neither God nor Jesus can be rescued from the mire, and it is a waste of energy to try. Some in this group use the term post-Christian in order to acknowledge that themes of liberation and revolution can come from the Christian tradition, but that the particular symbols and rituals around Jesus' death and resurrection are no longer liberating for women or anyone else. Womanist theologians form a fourth group that sees Jesus as a political Messiah, like Moses, who understands and supports the desires of oppressed groups for freedom and salvation. "To free humans from bondage was Jesus's own definition of his ministry."[22]

The witness of survivors of sexual abuse and the debate within womanist and feminist theology has led me to look again at the stories of Jesus' crucifixion and ask how they look from the perspective of those with little power in the Christian church. In this section I am asking how certain forms of Christian theology may actually contribute to the problem of clergy sexual abuse. In order to understand, we must be able to imaginatively place ourselves within the structure of these stories as they might be perceived by a survivor of sexual abuse. The purpose of this exercise is to discover how the commitment to love and justice can become distorted in the religious drama, and what must be changed so that the Christian church is a safe place for those who are vulnerable.

THEORIES OF ATONEMENT[23]

The death and resurrection of Jesus is held up in many traditions as the supreme example of God's unconditional and sacrificial love for the creation and is symbolized in the Eucharist. "No one has greater love than this, to lay down one's life for one's friends." (John 15:13).

In this characterization of the devine-human drama God is the father of Jesus and humans are the children of the promises made to and by Jesus. The quality of the relationship between God the parent and Jesus the child is central for our faith. Jesus reveals the perfect faith of a believer toward the creator of the universe.

The theory of substitutionary atonement.[24] In the substitutionary theory of atonement Jesus was the substitute sacrifice for humans who deserved to die for their sin and evil. Because humans are evil, God's original plan for creation was jeopardized. God designed a plan for Jesus to come down as a human to live and to die as a sinless sacrifice to save humanity from its own evil. Jesus' sacrificial death means that humans do not have to pay the full penalty for sin, but can be reconciled with God. Now, through the blood of Jesus, those who believe can be saved from the evil world. Those who do not confess Jesus will be destroyed in an apocalypse as they deserve. One of the texts for substitutionary atonement is 1 Timothy 2:5, "There is one God; there is also one mediator between God and humankind, Christ Jesus, himself human, who gave himself as a ransom for all."[25]

The structure of this theory mirrors the patriarchal family. The father is all-loving and all-powerful; the children are guilty. There is nothing the children can do to earn mercy and no moral basis on which to make appeal to the love of the Father, because their sin and guilt is so overwhelming. The Father's rage is justified because of the disobedience and disloyalty of the children. No matter how they are treated by the Father, it is their own fault, and they must carry the blame for whatever the Father decides to do with them.

The guilt of the children is made worse by the existence of a perfect child who gave up his life for his siblings. He proves that the Father is just after all. If the guilty children repent of their sins, pledge total obedience to the reborn sibling, and agree to become submissive to the all-knowing Father, there is a chance they will not have to die a violent death like their brother.

One of the many problems with the theory of substitutionary atonement in relation to the issue of sexual violence is the image of the abusive God against which the children of creation have no power or moral claim. The omnipotence and perfection of God creates a unilateral relationship in which humans are in constant danger from an enraged God. The only protection is for the children to be submissive and obedient to God by praising the father and the son and living sanctified lives.

The theory of incarnational atonement. In this theory, the wrathful image of God is replaced by an emphasis on God's mercy and love toward the creation. God voluntarily suffers on behalf of the children of creation. The problem in human history is not the wrath of God but the self-destructive nature of sin and evil.

In their prideful arrogance humans try to be gods by creating institutions of great power. But because they do not acknowledge the sovereignty of God, these human creations become destructive, causing great suffering for everyone. Without the intervention of God's power and love, the creation is doomed to annihilation, and the signs of this possibility are ever present for those who have eyes to see.

God is not angry, but saddened, by the evil of humanity. God sees that human sin is destructive and eventually everything will be destroyed. In this theory, God is not directly abusive but is more like the non-offending parent, the one who cannot stop the violence because divine action would curtail human freedom. So God faces a dilemma. How can God respond to the evil of humans without being destructive?[26]

In the incarnation, God comes to earth in human form. In Jesus, who came as a baby and grew into a powerful healer and preacher, God communicates a message of love. By loving the outcasts and confronting those in power, Jesus models a form of power that is not destructive, but redemptive. Those who perceive and follow Jesus are those who can love as he loves.

The climax of the story comes when Jesus is faced with the organized principalities and powers of the world and has to decide how to respond. At this point God, in the form of Jesus, chooses suffering over violence and goes to the cross in order to reveal that love is more powerful than hate. "In Christ God was reconciling the world to himself, not counting their trespasses against them and entrusting the message of reconciliation to us. So we are ambassadors for Christ." (2 Cor 5:19)

The witness of Jesus is made even more powerful by the fact that God's presence among humans is absolutely voluntary. There was no compulsion or obligation on God's part to make such a sacrifice to save humanity. Rather, in God's total freedom, God chose to suffer with the creation in order to bring salvation. For the children who recognize the reality of God in Jesus, there is new life and new power to actualize love in history. For those children who remain stubborn in their prideful sin, self-destructive consequences follow, and the tragedy of history continues.

The theory of incarnational atonement seems designed to deal explicitly with the problem of the abusive God. By turning from an emphasis on wrath and sacrifice to an emphasis on suffering and imitation, God is presented as compassionate, and love is seen as more powerful than violence.

However, in terms of what we are learning from survivors of sexual violence, this theory also has problems. While a benevolent parent seems preferable to one who is abusive, the patriarchal structure of the relationship is fully intact. God is the perfect parent who intervenes in history to save the disloyal and disobedient children. God has the power to give and take life, and God unilaterally decides to institute the incarnation as the revelation of divine reality. The children are helpless until they are rescued by the omnipotent God. The children are morally corrupt until they are saved by the perfect God. The unilateral power relationship between God and humans is fully maintained. God has the power to be abusive, but God freely chooses instead to suffer in response to the evil of creation.

In addition, the emphasis on a suffering God is highly problematic for many survivors of sexual violence. By this theology they feel they have been encouraged to suffer abuse in silence without seeking justice for their mistreatment. While women and children are suffering in silence, male perpetrators of sexual violence are leaders in society without accountability for their crimes. There is something wrong with an omnipotent God who encourages victims to suffer in silence for the evil of others. There is something wrong with an innocent Jesus who suffers because of the evil of the leaders of his society. Such a view ignores the cries for justice from the vulnerable, while the powerful maintain their privilege and abusive behaviors.[27]

CLERGY SEXUAL ABUSE AS A FORM OF INCEST

Now I want to turn specifically to the dynamics of clergy sexual abuse and ask how this phenomenon plays out the church's theology. Religious rituals and beliefs that are practiced over many years become models which consciously and unconsciously influence our inner reality. Figures in these dramas become internal objects that organize our religious experiences. The views of atonement I have described organize the religious imagination in particular ways: we can identify with an all-powerful, all-knowing, and all-loving God; we can identify with Jesus who takes on the sins of humanity, submits his will to God's, and sacrifices his life unto death on the cross for the sake of the relationship. In this distorted family drama, perhaps the Holy Spirit is like the non-offending parent who has been silenced or is colluding, a third figure for identification. Survivors of incest are clear about the enforced roles in their family dramas. An incest victim submits to the will of her father, takes on the guilt for any sin involved, and sacrifices her life and talents for the sake of the relationship. Her father has put himself in the role of God who is all-powerful, all-knowing, and all-loving, and whose decisions and values cannot be questioned. The mother is often silenced by her husband. Thus the religious drama is acted out as a family drama.

Religious leaders and ordained minsters are the authoritative interpreters of the drama between God and humanity. What we say in prayers and sermons, how we act out the rituals of the Eucharist and other sacraments, and how we practice the ministries of the church, are all expressions of our theology. Conservative and evangelical traditions connect the authority and power of God directly with obedience and submission for humans. Liberal and progressive traditions emphasize the love of God and the service of humans toward one another within the context of God's pure motives and behaviors. However, the choice between a punitive or benevolent patriarch is not a real choice. Conservative traditions define power as hierarchy and Christians are commanded to be subservient and obedient to God, the church, and the clergy. There is no mystification about the definition and exercise of power. But liberal images of God as a benevolent patriarch can be dangerous. It is not enough to submit and serve God. One must have a transformation of heart and soul. One must love God, internalize the hierarchical relationship itself, and call it mutuality. But how does anyone have mutuality with a

God who is all-good, all-powerful, and all-knowing? Only by repressing any rebellion against such a God. Conservative churches demand and enforce obedience. Liberal churches want expectations written onto the soul. In situations of clergy sexual abuse, such religion is not only a rape of the body, it is a soul-murder.[28]

The clergyman is a representative of God and an interpreter of the mysteries of the Eucharist. Persons who want to know God and who seek healing come in trust and in the quest for salvation. Conservative traditions give altar calls for repentance and commitment to Christ. Liberal traditions are more likely to invite persons to join in intimate conversation about their deepest thoughts. Pastoral counseling is a specialized form of this invitation in which long-term covenants are formed for spiritual direction and deep inner healing.

The most common scenario of clergy sexual abuse is a male clergyman with a female parishioner or with a child. What happens when pastors and counselors sexualize their ministry relationships? The result is a form of incest. A sexual relationship between a male clergyman and a female parishioner replicates the dynamics of the drama between a patriarchal God and an obedient, self-sacrificing Jesus standing in for a sinful humanity. A relationship that was supposedly based on the healing needs of the parishioner becomes reversed so that the parishioner serves the sexual needs of the clergyman. In religious terms, the clergyman has taken the place of God who is all-knowing, all-powerful, and all-loving, and the parishioner has taken the place of Jesus who takes on the sins of humanity, submits her will to God's, and sacrifices her life unto death on the cross for the sake of the relationship

What is wrong with the incest of clergy sexual abuse? It exploits the inequality between men and women (and often between adults and children) under the guise of mutuality and pseudo-intimacy. A relationship which is inherently unequal, in which a man is the representative of a loving and powerful God and a woman the representative of a broken and dying humanity, becomes the occasion for exploitation. A relationship in which God's love and justice is supposed to be a force for healing in the world is distorted into the sacrifice of the world for a broken and evil God. This theological drama is painful enough when it is used by Christian fathers and clergymen to justify their abusive behaviors. But the survivors of sexual abuse are saying more. They are saying that an abusive God and abusive clergymen do not contradict the church's theology. The images of abuse are inherent in the symbols themselves. A church that preaches God's love but projects the evil of the world onto women and other marginalized groups is preaching an abusive God. There is a connection between clergy abuse of power and images of an abusive God.

> People, who have power to dominate others and wish to maintain that status quo, profit by a God who legitimates the exercise of power.... Moreover, they profit by a God who possesses these characteristics himself in divine measure.[29]

An all-powerful God controls everything that happens; sexual abuse is total control of the spiritual life of another. An all-knowing God knows what is best for others; sexual abuse is often rationalized as a form of superior and special knowledge. An all-loving God makes no mistakes in evaluating the needs of others; sexual abuse is often justified as a loving relationship. Against the power of God, there is no effective defense. We must submit to such a God in obedience and service. This matches the actual vulnerability of many persons who seek out a pastor or pastoral counselor for spiritual guidance. When a minister responds with sexual abuse, the crucifixion is reenacted. One woman put her religious witness in a poem entitled "Good New for Modern Man, Bad News for Modern Woman":[30]

> In the name of the Father and of the Son,
> and of the Holy Spirit. Amen.
>
> Our Father who are in heaven,
> Hallowed be Thy name...
>
> Faith of our Fathers living still...
> Of the Father's love begotten.
>
> Liturgical melodies weave in and out
> Causing patriarchy to be sacred.
>
> Unspoken, unlabeled actions go sin free,
> While the guiltless continue their confessions.
>
> Children of the heavenly Father
> Become baptized, sealed with a cross.

Whose sacrifice is this?

Women weep at the sight of Christ on the cross.
Offenses to God are remembered.

The words of institution are said.
Wine and bread are offered.

The blood of Christ shed for you.
The body of Christ given for you.

Whose blood is shed? Whose body is given?

Sermons blast at the core of humanity
Framed in sexist slanted language.

The raped become convicted
The molested become ashamed.

The perpetrator escorts his family out
Relieved by his perfunctory participation.

Whose betrayal is this?

In the name of the Mother, and of the Daughter,
And of the Holy Spirit.

Have mercy on us. Amen. (Lorraine Frampton, 1992)

WHERE IS THE HOPE?

Clergy sexual abuse is an expression rather than an aberration of fairly traditional forms of theology. How do we conceptualize God and humanity so that the vulnerable are protected?

The search is on in many places for non-abusive images of God that humans can relate to in partnership and mutual accountability. I have been working with the image of a relational, ambiguous God. Such a God cannot be all-powerful, all-knowing and all-loving because then faith can only be obedience and submission. A fully relational God includes the suffering of everyone, including survivors who have been silenced by society. The whole world is in God's hands. A fully relational God is resilient for justice in the face of moral ambiguity, like the persistence of

41

the widow who seeks justice from the judge. The central problem is how to conceptualize the love and power of God in relational terms that give us a more adequate model for human relationships.

> Humans have the power to nurture or abuse others. In order for evil to be overcome, we must face the tendency in ourselves and in others to use power in evil ways. When we face the depth of our own ambiguity, we will discover the resilient hope that power can be used with justice. Only as we confess the abuse of power in our own lives, confront the abuse of power in others, repent of its evil, and commit ourselves anew to justice and righteousness, will the possibility of evil be contained.[31]

The integrity of pastoral counseling as a ministry of the church depends on a theological critique of our own interests, that is, our ability to see how our privilege and abusive patterns become embodied in our personal theologies and counseling practices. Clergy sexual abuse is not just a confusion about sexuality by pastoral counselors who have not worked through their countertransference issues. The abusive patterns of ten to twenty percent of clergy who sexually abuse women and children cannot be explained by individualistic psychological analysis. Rather, clergy sexual abuse is a theological problem. It is an enactment of the image of an abusive God that is too frequently proclaimed from the pulpits and sacristies of our churches. Survivors of clergy sexual abuse are calling for a new reformation in the life of the church. It is from survivors that the church will discover the new images of God that can bring healing and transformation for all persons.

Let me close with a witness from my friend Janet, who was raped at ten and later seduced by her professor when she was a seminary student.

> And the circle goes 'round, but this time, it is being renamed. Life is redefined with new boundaries, new safe places. Experiences include marital patience, family's validation, shared stories with others, healing hugs, sobs that reek of pain and the christening tears that name the new reality. Hurt and shame transform themselves into strength and the assurance of the resurrected life.

The future of our religious communities depends on hearing and believing the witness of Janet on behalf of the thousands of others who have suffered at the hands of clergy and whose story has never been heard. Those of us who are pastoral counselors have a special vocation to hear the new religious witness of survivors of sexual abuse. Careful listening to our own suffering and the suffering of others has been an important theme of the pastoral care movement. It is time to join in a new reformation that is occurring among us and in our society.

CHAPTER 4

THE SOCIO-POLITICAL CONTEXT

James N. Poling

𝕿his chapter I dedicate to Carol, Janet, Karen and countless others whose lives and ministries have been forever changed by abusive clergymen. I acknowledge and thank the many survivors of sexual violence who are pastoral counselors. May God give them the strength to speak the truth so that the church can be liberated from its silence and complicity. I acknowledge the presence of clergy abusers in the pastoral counseling movement. I know their pain. I have acted out my fear and rage on those who are vulnerable. I want them to know that liberation is a real possibility, but first we must repent, make public confession, begin restitution, and get help so the vulnerable are safe with us. Our behaviors have damaged many individuals, as well as the religious and professional communities we profess to love. I plead with all to stop the abuse and begin to make pastoral counseling and the churches safe places for all in their woundedness, without fear of being abused again.[32]

The initial estimates of the prevalence of clergy sexual abuse are astounding. Marie Fortune of The Center for the Prevention of Sexual and Domestic Violence says they have received notice of over 1,000 cases in ten years.[33] Other estimates are suggesting that 10-25% of male clergy have engaged in sexual behaviors with parishioners.[34] *The Christian Century* has recorded dozens of cases in the last few years. There are many thousands of cases nationwide. Apparently, clergy sexual abuse is a problem in white, black and other ethnic religious communities.

For the purpose of this discussion, I define clergy sexual abuse in the following way: Clergy sexual misconduct occurs whenever a member of the clergy engages in sexual behaviors with someone for whom he or she has spiritual responsibility.

Ordination is the Christian church's[35] authorization for religious leadership in a particular tradition and the sanction that such a person is trustworthy with the innermost struggles of a person's spiritual life. It is the minister's role to lead persons to God through Jesus Christ and to the healing resources of the church as the Body of Christ. Whenever a clergyperson uses the office of minister or counselor to make himself/ herself, rather than Christ, the object of admiration and attachment, that act is a violation of trust and a betrayal of the role of pastor.[36] No theology supports a sexual relationship as a valid form of ministry. One cannot be a pastor or pastoral counselor to an individual and at the same time a sexual partner. Consent is not a defense when one of the persons is a member of the clergy and one is a parishioner or counselee. The minister has authority and responsibility for what happens in the pastoral relationship, and sexual violations are wrong.

The pastoral counseling movement has generated a lot of literature about intimacy and sexuality that offers psychological explanations for clergy sexual abuse. This approach conflicts with recent feminist and womanist literature that emphasizes power and calls the same behaviors "clergy abuse." While these two approaches are not necessarily contradictory, they do represent conflicting political positions on what is happening and what the church should do. It is my thesis that the church in general and the pastoral counseling movement in particular has failed to understand the real problem which the feminist and womanist challenge clarifies and this has failed to address the sexual abusers of clergy.

As long as churches and synagogues understand abuses by male clergy as disorders of intimacy and sexuality, without attending to a social analysis of male dominance and violence, the church is unlikely to move decisively to stop abuse. In fact, the churches will more likely continue to blame the victims and excuse abusive pastors. In the main part of this article, I will examine the womanist and feminist analysis of male sexual violence in society, then apply this analysis to the church and clergy sexual abuse. My assumption is that clergy sexual abuse is a part of the larger reality of systematic male violence toward women.

EXCURSIONS ON MY ACCOUNTABILITY

First, however, I need to address the issue of my accountability as a white male. It is time for men to join women who are speaking out against clergy sexual abuse and to disclose the damage that has been done to so many individuals, marriages, families, and congregations, and to the integrity of the ministry and the church. It is time for Euro-Americans to join African-Americans to understand the way race, gender, and class create systems of oppression that conceal the violence of male sexual abuse toward women and children. As we become aware of the magnitude of this problem, we will realize that everyone must join in political solidarity with those who are already resisting and together we must challenge the way power is currently used and abused in the church.

I speak today out of my own experience. In my early ministry, I was not concerned about sexual violence or clergy sexual abuse. I was writing about practical theology, aging, theological method and ethics. My first piece on sexual abuse in the family was written in 1988. Before then, I was a part of the silent conspiracy about the sexual violence of men.

I gradually began to wake up:

— by listening to black and white seminary students describe their abusive experiences in families and churches;

— by working with feminist therapists and supervisors who confronted my complicity, and

— by conversation with womanist and feminist colleagues who took time to challenge my false consciousness.

I have reached the point where not speaking is more painful than the vulnerability of speaking. But even in speaking about violence against women, men can make things more dangerous for women. Every time I write something else on this topic, I drift back to my pre-feminist male-dominant mode. I reassert my privileged position as a white, heterosexual, educated, professional male without awareness of what I am doing.[37]

Under what conditions can I as a white male speak about this issue when I have inherited and participated in a tradition of male cover-up and collusion? Several principles are important whenever white men write about issues of abuse:

— We must respond to the authoritative stories of black and white women.

— We must rely on feminist and womanist methods of analysis which challenge male socialization and power.

— We must have regular structures of accountability to women who have the power to challenge and change sexist distortions.

PSYCHOLOGICAL INTERPRETATIONS
OF CLERGY SEXUALITY

Pastoral counseling literature has been leading the way with interpretations of clergy sexual abuse as a problem of intimacy and sexuality. Two examples will illustrate my point. Notice the images and explanations of clergy sexual behaviors with members of their churches.

One article began: "Less than a year following a divorce, a minister committed professional suicide by becoming sexually involved with a married woman in his congregation."[38] The authors used other examples that purport to illustrate the problem of "the resurgence of the erotic" in the midst of crisis. The thesis is that the crisis of loss often leads to erotic attachments which are sometimes inappropriate. The minister who was sexually involved with a parishioner was presented as someone with unresolved grief because of a divorce. This very description leads the reader away from issues of abuse and attempts to develop psychological explanations of crisis and sexuality.

In the same issue of this journal another author explored the "distortions of relationships between male pastors and their female parishioners":

> In an age when intimacy is so eagerly pursued and yet so rarely enjoyed, the pastor who is sensitive, empathic, and attentive to parishioners sometimes unexpectedly finds the gift of human warmth and presence complicated by Cupid's arrows. "How do we protect the pastoral relationship from romantic and sexual contamination without sacrificing the heart-to-heart relationships with Christ's people which is the wellspring of true ministry"?[39]

While this author attempted to address ethical violations of clergy, he defined the problem psychologically as an issue of countertransference and misplaced sexuality rather than politically as abuse related to patriarchy. Sexual involvement "just happens" whenever people are intimate. The central question of the author is how we can prevent "romantic and sexual contamination" in ministry, not how we can prevent male pastors from abusing their power.

Other examples would make the point that when pastoral counselors offer psychological explanations of clergy sexual behaviors without power analysis of gender relationships and social constructions of sexuality, issues of abuse disappear into the background. Both articles admit that some clergy sexual behaviors are problematic, but neither makes an effort to understand the damage from the perspective of victims. Rather, the problem is analyzed from the perspective of the minister as an intrapsychic one of managing libido or sexual energy and thus accepts and reinforces the abusive and classist structures.

THE FEMINIST AND WOMANIST INTERPRETATIONS OF SEXUAL ABUSE

Now I turn to the womanist and feminist analysis of male sexual violence in society to help us understand the roots of clergy sexual abuse. The womanist and feminist interpretations of male violence against women begin with the recognition of inequality and oppression of women under patriarchy. It is crucial to understand the ideology of male dominance as a constant reality of women's experience. Listen to Adrienne Rich's definition:

> Patriarchy is the power of the fathers: ... a system in which men ... determine what part women shall or shall not play, and in which the female is everywhere subsumed under the male.... Whatever my status or situation, my derived economic class, or my sexual preference, I live under the power of the fathers, and I have access only to so much of privilege or influence as patriarchy is willing to accede to me, and only for so long as I will pay the price for male approval.[40]

According to bell hooks, patriarchy must be understood as a system of oppression interlocked with racism.

> In a retrospective examination of the black female slave experience, sexism looms as large as racism as an oppressive force in the lives of black women. Institutionalized sexism — that is, patriarchy — formed

the base of the American social structure along with racial imperialism.[41]

One of the methods of these interlocking oppressions is violence, especially rape, incest, and other forms of sexual violence. The fear of rape is an ever-present reality for all women. There is constant danger that a woman can be assaulted in the streets, within her acquaintance circle, or within her family. It is not necessary that all men rape in order for women to be terrorized. The reality of rape itself creates terror for women, according to Susan Brownmiller and Hester Eisenstein.

> In the minds of women, the knowledge of the possibility of rape act[s] as a powerful form of social control. To keep this knowledge alive, it [is] not necessary for all men to rape all women. This work could be carried out by only a few men.... "[M]en who commit rape have served in effect as front-line masculine shock troops, terrorist guerrillas in the longest sustained war the world has ever known."[42]

However, bell hooks again argues that analysis of racism leads to a more complex understanding of how the facts of sexual violence affect the imagination of the American psyche.

> As far back as slavery, white people established a social hierarchy based on race and sex that ranked white men first, white women second, though sometimes equal to black men, who are ranked third, and black women last. What this means in terms of the sexual politics of rape is that if one white woman is raped by a black man, it is seen as more important, more significant than if thousands of black women are raped by one white man.[43]

This tangle of racial and sexual politics creates the male-dominant family. The answer of society to the violence of rape is male protection through possession. A woman is required to subordinate herself to a man in the family or through marriage, supposedly in order to be protected against the possibility of rape in the streets. But as we are slowly learning, marriages and families are actually the most dangerous places for women. More women are raped within the family than outside the family.[44] So male protection is not protection, but it is domination. Families and marriages are primary institutions for terrorizing and enforcing female subordination to men through sexual violence.[45]

The oppression of women is also enforced through economic exploitation. Most women are forced to marry *and* work in low-paying jobs. In modern society most women are employed in horizontally stratified jobs at the bottom of the economic pyramid, "as secretaries, domestics, nurses, typists, telephone operators, child-care workers, waitresses."[46] The denial of employment and educational opportunities for women through many complex subterfuges means that most women are stuck with the jobs they have and cannot afford to challenge the way they are treated. This also forces them into marriage in order to have adequate support for themselves and their children. Racism, sexism, and classism combine especially to exploit women of color. According to bell hooks and other scholars, racial solidarity does not protect women of color from the sexist oppression of male violence.[47] The economic exploitation of African American women often leads to increased vulnerability to sexist violence. Women who manage to rise above the working class to the professions still find themselves in male-dominated institutions where sexual harassment and exploitation is common.

According to feminists and womanists, patriarchal forces of violence and economic exploitation are interlocked with another form of patriarchal oppression, what Catherine MacKinnon in *Sexual Harassment of Working Women* calls "the sexualization of women."[48] This same point is explored in Toni Morrison's *Race-ing, Justice, En-gender-ing Power.* In order to survive, women have to accommodate to the patriarchal system that control their labor and sexuality. Men have power over women, and thus the arrangements are set for sexual harassment and exploitation. Adrienne Rich summarizes

> Economically disadvantaged, women — whether waitresses or professors — endure sexual harassment to keep their jobs and learn to behave in a complacently and ingratiatingly heterosexual manner because they discover this is their true qualification for employment, whatever the job description.... The fact is that the workplace, among other social institutions, is a place where women have learned to accept male violation of

our psychic and physical boundaries as the price of survival.[49]

The consequences of the patriarchal system are that women's labor is sexualized and women's subordination is eroticized.[50] This means that men, by conscious and unconscious design, use their power to maintain their dominance, and men are socialized to find the exercise of power in relation to the vulnerability of women to be an erotic experience. What is organized by patriarchy as a system of power and domination becomes internalized as male sexual desire, which is then projected onto women through obsessions and fantasies. Men who reject this socialization are considered a threat to patriarchy. Again, Catherine MacKinnon:

> What if inequality is built into the social conceptions of male and female sexuality, of masculinity and femininity, of sexiness and heterosexual attractiveness? Incidents of sexual harassment suggest that male sexual desire itself may be aroused by female vulnerability.... Men feel they can take advantage, so they want to, so they do.[51]

According to feminist and womanist scholars, patriarchy is a system in which sexualization, violence and economic exploitation are interlocked in a way that enables male abusers to exploit women in the family, at work and everywhere. Over a third of female children are molested and over half of all women experience rape or attempted rape. Only a small percentage of abusers ever face consequences such as censure, exposure or jail for their crimes. According to Diane Russell, less than one percent of rapists and child molesters are arrested and convicted of a crime.[52] In analyzing the secrecy of the majority of rapes in American society, Angela Davis asks this provocative question:

> Where are the anonymous rapists? ... Might not this anonymity be a privilege enjoyed by men whose status protects them from prosecution? ... It seems, in fact, that men of the capitalist class and their middle-class partners are immune to prosecution because they commit their sexual assaults with the same unchallenged authority that legitimizes their daily assaults on the labor

and dignity of working people.... The class structure of capitalism encourages men who wield power in the economic and political realm to become routine agents of sexual exploitation.[53]

The reason why anonymous rapists are not brought to justice is that "their status protects them from prosecution." Disclosure of how many men of high status and privilege have raped and exploited women would reveal that patriarchy is built on exploitation. Patriarchy is a system of sexual and economic exploitation of women, and the men who manage and profit from this system are protected.

In summary, the feminist and womanist argument, as I understand it, is that patriarchy is enforced through a combination of forces including economic exploitation, violence, and the sexualization of women. It is this system that begins to explain sexual terrorism in rape, incest, and professional sexual abuse. Sexual exploitation is not an aberration of an otherwise fair and just system of commerce and interpersonal relationships. Rather, sexual violence is an integral part of a patriarchal, capitalistic system that is based on the subordination of women and children, and which is interlocked with the oppression of people of color, the poor, gays and lesbians and other groups.

At a time when women are challenging patriarchy on many fronts, violent assaults and sexual and economic exploitation of women are increasing. Being able to understand and describe how patriarchy expresses itself through sexual violence against women is a step toward destroying this system which turns women into victims and men into perpetrators.

UNDERSTANDING SEXUAL ABUSE BY CLERGY

In this section I will explore issues in the white Christian churches because that is the foundation of my experience. I urge persons from other traditions to make similar explorations of other traditions. Now I turn to an exploration of how clergy sexual abuse in the church is an expression of the same patriarchal system I have been discussing. That the Christian church is patriarchal has been well established by Mary Daly, Rosemary Ruether, Carter Heyward, Gerda Lerner, and many others.[54] Patriarchy is presupposed by and is basic to the explicit teaching and theology of Christianity. Many churches in the world still forbid the ordination of women and identify the male-dominant, heterosexual family with God's perfect will for creation. The progressive churches have begun to examine their patriarchal ideology and practices in the past twenty years, but only the smallest progress has been made. Look at the relative percentages of male and female clergy and pastoral counselors, the balance of male and female leadership, and the organization of local churches. While we pride ourselves in the white, liberal churches on recent progress, we are a long way from actually changing the patriarchal assumptions that underlie our practices. Male dominance in the black churches seems to be equally well established.

In the male-dominant church, the volunteer labor of women has been and continues to be exploited. Historically, male leadership has controlled the church, and women have served in subordinate capacities, usually in volunteer positions. Volunteerism in the church is actually a euphemism for the work of women. In some places, women make up 60-75% of the membership of local congregations, and what gets done in the churches is primarily done by women. A church dominated by male clergy, teachers, theologians, and bureaucrats, but dependent on the volunteer labor of women, is an exact mirror of modern, industrial society and is also replicated in the theological dynamics of the atonement.

In the last few years the struggle for ordination by women represents a demand for equal power and leadership in the church, and a demand that women receive equal pay for equal work. It is ironic and tragic that during this time of active liberation movements for women, the white, liberal churches are experiencing severe problems with declining membership and declining funds. Sometimes it seems clear that as women demand equal power and leadership, men are withdrawing their presence and their money in protest. Some women are also losing interest in the church and going where they can live with integrity and meaning. The rise in the popularity of the conservative churches that are more explicitly patriarchal during this same time period may well be one way the liberation actions of women are being resisted.

In the male-dominant church, women have been and continue to be sexualized. Numerous scholars have documented how Augustine and other theologians defined women as subordinate and considered their sexuality a danger to men.[55] Euro-American theology has identified women's sexuality as evil and man's rationality as good and established a hierarchy that is defined as God's natural order. In the last decades we have been through a "sexual revolution" whose explicit goal is liberation from dualistic and hierarchical thinking based on gender. This has given some space for women to explore their sexuality as a positive reality.[56] But it has also given men permission to assert their sexual desires more forcefully, often at the expense of women. Again, bell hooks:

> As long as women were divided into two groups, virgin women who were the 'good' girls and sexually permissive women who were the 'bad' girls, men were able to maintain some semblance of caring for women. Now that the pill and other contraceptive devices give men unlimited access to the bodies of women, they have ceased to feel that it is at all necessary to show women any consideration or respect. They can now see all women as 'bad,' as 'whores,' and openly reveal their contempt and hatred.[57]

This process of increased sexualization of women means that women who are called to lay or ordained leadership in the church are subject to greater vulnerability. Men sexualize interaction with women in order to gain power. While women have seized the opportunity to liberate themselves, many male leaders have increased their obsession with sexuality, which often leads to abuse.

In the male-dominant church, women and children have been and continue to be victimized by sexual abuse. Ten years ago there was silence about clergy sexual abuse; now, hardly a week goes by without some new disclosure.[58] Some of this is a result of the abuse by clergy that has always existed. Every century has its examples — from Luther's appeal that the church should support the dependents of celibate clergy rather than force them to live in poverty, to the Wesley affairs,[59] to the scandals surrounding Paul Tillich and Jimmy Swaggart. But I suspect abuse is also increasing in response to the womanist and feminist challenge. Men are escalating their abusive behaviors in response to the ambitions of women. It is interesting that during this same time, rape, incest, sexual harassment, and violence against gays and lesbians has increased. I believe that clergy sexual abuse is a part of this same backlash against the liberation of women with the purpose of the reassertion of male dominance. Part of the function of abuse, as we have seen, is to terrorize women so that they remain in a subordinate position and cease and desist in their demands for equality. Many complainants about clergy sexual abuse are women who are training for ministry and other forms of religious leadership in the church. As I review the dozens of cases of clergy sexual abuse I have heard about personally, I am astounded at the number of women whose careers have been damaged or derailed because they were abused by mentors serving as gatekeepers of the church's power.

What situations are more dangerous for women than pastoral counseling, pastoral care, spiritual direction, and ministry supervision? In these situations, the man is usually the one in the power position, and the agreement involves sharing of life's most intimate personal, sexual, and spiritual issues. The church claims direct access to the God of the universe who has a personal destiny for each person and community. By virtue of ordination, education, experience and leadership, male clergy are the keepers of these resources. Pastors, church leaders, scholars, teachers, and counselors have become the gatekeepers of this information for women as they assert their right to know for themselves. Given the feminist and womanist analysis of patriarchy, situations of ministry training and supervision create significant danger for women.

This brings us to Angela Davis' haunting question: Where are the anonymous rapists? Why is the church silent when charges of clergy sexual abuse are brought, and why is there so much resistance to hearing the demands of women? Some readers may object, saying that churches everywhere are making great strides in this area. But for every notorious case in which decisive action has been taken, there are at least ten cases in which the church has dragged its feet and blamed women for causing trouble. Every policy and procedure that has been developed so far is organized as much or more to protect the church's reputation and insurance as to respond to the systemic issues of sexual abuse within a patriarchal church.[60] We have a long way to go before the depths of this issue will be faced by the church. Meanwhile, the majority of male clergy who have abused female parishioners, clients, and supervisees continue their ministries without penalty.

This brings us back to an earlier point. I pointed out the tension between psychological interpretations of clergy sexual abuse as a problem of intimacy and sexuality versus political interpretations by womanists and feminists that these are issues of power and abuse. I suggested that perhaps these interpretations were not necessarily contradictory but may suggest different directions for the church. But after the analysis about how male dominance, exploitation of labor and sexual violence are interrelated, I would go further and suggest that interpreting clergy sexual abuse in psychological terms is actually part of the cover-up of abuse and the protection of abusers. Patriarchy depends on the process of mystification, that is, hiding the ideological and institutional powers at work in what can be misconstrued as interpersonal relationships. So one of the issues is whether the field of pastoral theology and counseling will cast its lot with feminists and womanists who are demanding change or continue its covert collusion with the powers of oppression and violence.

Where are the anonymous rapists? They are the same leaders who benefit from the church as it is. The power that enables male clergy to exploit women sexually and in other ways is the same power that protects them from the consequences of their crimes. One abuser I know threatened to bring down the whole church if he were held accountable for his crimes. And he could act on his threats because he knew the secrets of so many other leaders. This example suggests that men who challenge or defect from patriarchy are also in danger from the violence and domination of those who will defend their privilege and power at all costs. Male collusion for protection is a real culprit in maintaining the silence and inaction of the church. Men must find the courage to defect from the patriarchal system of the church and stop their collusion and protection. God bless the women and men who resist with all their strength and challenge the church to live up to its promise of live and justice for all.

CONCLUSIONS

1. One of the functions of sexual violence is to enforce patriarchy and keep women in subordinate positions. This analogy suggests that clergy sexual abuse serves as a deterrent and danger to women who seek ordination and other forms of leadership in the church.

2. Clergy sexual abuse will not dramatically change until there is gender equality and an end to patriarchy. While policies and procedures are requirements of justice, the deeper socio-political roots have to be addressed and power reconfigured before abuse will be stopped.

3. Clergy sexual abuse is an issue of power and patriarchy and not just an issue of intimacy and sexuality. As power is acknowledged and gender constructed beyond patriarchy, issues of sexuality will be transformed. In the meantime, intrapsychic and interpersonal construc-tions of intimacy and sexuality that do not include social analysis will continue to be a part of the cover-up and an ideological mystification in service to patriarchy.

We must press on with courage to understand the deficits that have gotten us to this point. Patriarchy and racism are systems that are infused through the theology and practices of white, black and other ethnic churches, as well as conservative, liberal, and radical forms of Christianity. As long as we deny the oppression of women, people of color, the poor, lesbians and gays, and those with disabilities, and as long as we worship a God imaged as a patriarchal power, we will also tolerate the behaviors of male clergy to abuse their power.

ENDNOTES

[1]Holroyd and Brodsky, cited in Richard Allen Blackmon, *The Hazards of the Ministry*. Unpublished Ph.D. dissertation. (Pasadena, CA: Fuller Theological Seminary, 1984).

[2]Richard Allen Blackmon, *The Hazards of the Ministry*. Unpublished Ph.D. dissertation. (Pasadena, CA: Fuller Theological Seminary, 1984).

[3]For further discussion see Marie Fortune, *Is Nothing Sacred? When Sex Invades the Pastoral Relationship* (San Francisco, CA: Harper & Row, 1989).

[4]Frederick W. Keene, "Structures of Forgiveness in the New Testament," Unpublished paper, 1993. P. 2.

[5]*Ibid.*, p. 10.

[6]Fortune, *Op. cit.*

[7]Kathe A. Stark, "Child Sexual Abuse in the Catholic Church," in Schoener, et al. (Eds.), *Psychotherapists' Sexual Involvement with Clients* (Minneapolis, MN: Walk-In Counseling Center, 1989).

[8]Don Clark, "Sexual Abuse in the Church; The Law Steps In," *Christian Century*, 1993, Vol. 110, No. 12.

[9]William White, *Incest in the Organization* (Bloomington, IL: Lighthouse Training Institute, 1986).

[10]Marie Fortune, *Is Nothing Sacred? When Sex Invades the Pastoral Relationship* (San Francisco, CA: Harper & Row, 1989); *Sexual Violence: The Unmentionable Sin: An Ethical and Pastoral Perspective* (New York: Pilgrim Press, 1983).

[11]While the majority of victims are women and girls, a significant number of men and boys are also victims of clergy sexual abuse.

[12]The estimate of 10 to 20 percent is increasingly used in the literature and is based on preliminary research. See Peter Rutter, *Sex in the*

Forbidden Zone (Los Angeles, CA: Jeremy Tarcher, 1986), p. 36; Lloyd Rediger, *Ministry and Sexuality* (Minneapolis, MN: Fortress Press, 1990), p. 2; R.T. Brock and H.C. Lukens, "Affair Prevention in the Ministry," *Journal of Psychology and Christianity*, 1989, Vol. 4, pp. 44-55.

[13]Charles V. Gerkin, "On the Art of Caring," *The Journal of Pastoral Care*, 1991, Vol. 46, No. 4, p. 400.

[14]"The aim of the study is to formulate questions directed at religious leaders, so that their teachings may offer liberating perspectives to women and children as well as men." Annie Imbens and Ineke Jonker, *Christianity and Incest* (Minneapolis, MN: Fortress Press, 1992). P. 1.

[15]*Ibid.*, p. 6.

[16]*Ibid.*, p. 217.

[17]*Ibid.*, p. 66.

[18]*Ibid.*, p. 41.

[19]*Ibid.*, p. 209.

[20]*Ibid.*, p. 271.

[21]*Ibid.*, p. 278.

[22]Jacquelyn Grant, *White Women's Christ and Black Woman's Jesus* (Atlanta, GA: Scholars Press, 1989). P. 215.

[23]This section is taken from my book, *The Abuse of Power: A Theological Problem* (Nashville, TN: Abington Press, 1991), pp. 168-173, and is reprinted here with the permission of Abingdon Press. For summaries of theories of atonement, see Daniel Day Williams, *The Spirit and Forms of Love* (New York: Crossroad, 1988). Pp. 53ff; Joanne Carlson Brown and Carole R. Bohn (Eds.), *Christianity, Patriarchy and Abuse* (New York: Pilgrim Press, 1989), pp. 4ff.; Catherine Keller, *From a Broken Web* (New York: Beacon, 1986), pp. 164-165.

[24]Brown & Brohn, *Op. cit.*, pp. 7ff; Williams, *Op. cit.*, p. 175.

[25]Brock, *Op. cit.*, p. 55.

[26]Williams, *Op. cit.*, pp. 185-186.

[27]Brown & Bohn, *Op. cit.*, pp. 1ff.

[28]See the chapter on Freud's Schrebor in my book, *The Abuse of Power*, pp. 75-91.

[29]Imbens & Jonker, *Op. cit.*, p. 207.

[30]Lorraine Frampton, *Night Colors*. Unpublished D. Min. dissertation (Rochester, NY: Colgate Rochester Divinity School, 1993). P. 116.

[31]Poling, *Op. cit.*, p. 180.

[32]I especially thank Han van den Blink and the members of the Society for Pastoral Theology for their vision and support of my work on this topic. Their prayers, understanding, and support create the "loving context" in which I can do my work.

[33]*CPSDV Newsletter* (Seattle, WA: Center for the Prevention of Sexual and Domestic Violence, Fall 1992).

[34]See Marie Fortune, *Op. cit.*; G. Lloyd Rediger, *Ministry and Sexuality: Cases, Counseling, and Care* (Minneapolis, MN: Fortress, 1990); R.T. Brock and H.C. Lukens, "Affair Prevention in the Ministry," *Journal of Psychology and Christianity*, 1989, Vol. 8, No. 4, pp. 44-55.

[35]As in the previous chapter, I refer primarily to the Christian churches because of my own religious formation. However, I encourage others to explore their religious traditions for patriarchal assumptions and theologies that contribute to clergy sexual abuse.

[36]I am using masculine pronouns here because the majority of sexual abuse is done by male clergy. However, there are cases of sexual abuse by female clergy, and I am making no assumptions about the prevalence of other forms of abuse of power for both men and women.

[37]"The act of rape was paradigmatic of male attitudes toward women, if not in practice, then at least in theory. This did not mean ... all men wanted to rape women. But it did mean ... all men in some sense benefitted by their actions." Hester Eisenstein (quoting Susan Griffin), "Rape: The All-American Crime," in *Rape: Power of Consciousness* (San Francisco, CA: Harper & Row, 1979). P. 31.

[38]E. Wayne Hill, "The Resurgence of the Erotic in the Context of Loss: Implications for Pastoral Counseling," *The Journal of Pastoral Care*, 1992, Vol. 46, No. 3, p. 237.

[39]J. Steven Muse, "Faith, Hope and the 'Urge to Merge' in Pastoral Ministry: Some Countertransference-related Distortions of Relationships Between Male Pastors and Their Female Parishioners," *The Journal of Pastoral Care*, 1992, Vol. 46, No. 3, p. 299.

[40]Adrienne Rich, *Of Women Born: Motherhood as Experience and Institution* (New York: Norton, 1976), Pp. 57-58. For a womanist interpretation of patriarchy, see Audre Lorde, *Sister Outsider: Essays and Speeches by Audre Lorde* (New York: Crossing Press, 1984).

[41]bell hooks, *Ain't I a Woman?* (Boston: South End Press, 1981), P. 15.

[42]Hester Eisenstein (quoting Susan Brownmiller), *Against Our Will: Men, Women and Rape* (New York: Simon & Schuster, 1975), p. 30.

[43]hooks, *Op. cit.*, pp. 52-53.

[44]Diana Russell, *The Secret Trauma* (New York: Basic Books, 1986), p. 60.

[45]Hester Eisenstein (summarizing Susan Griffin), "Rape: The All-American Crime," *Ramparts*, 1971, Vol. 10, p. 31.

[46]Adrienne Rich, "Compulsory Heterosexuality and Lesbian Existence," in Elizabeth and Emily Abel (Eds.) *The Sign Reader: Women, Gender and Scholarship* (Chicago: University of Chicago Press, 1983), p. 149.

[47]bell hooks, *Ain't I a Woman?* (Boston: South End Press, 1981), p. 88.

[48]Adrienne Rich, "Compulsory Heterosexuality and Lesbian Existence," in (summarizing Catherine MacKinnon), *Sexual Harassment of Working Women* (New Haven, CT: Yale University Press, 1979), p. 149.

[49]Rich, *Op. cit.*, pp. 150-151.

[50]Rich, *Op. cit.*, p. 151

[51]Rich, *Op. cit.*, p. 151.

[52]Judith Herman, *Trauma and Recovery* (New York: Harper/Collins, 1992), p. 73; Diana Russell, *Sexual Exploitation: Rape, Child Sexual Abuse, and Sexual Harassment* (Beverly Hills, CA: Sage, 1984). The figures of child sexual abuse, adult rape, and law conviction rates all come from Diana Russell and related studies.

[53]Angela Davis, *Women, Race and Class* (New York: Vintage Books, 1983), pp. 199-200. For additional commentary on the relationship of sexual harassment, economic exploitation, and racial politics, see the following: Toni Morrison (Ed.), *Race-ing Justice, En-gender-ing Power: Essays on Anita Hill, Clarence Thomas, and the Construction of Social Reality* (New York: Pantheon Books, 1992); Robert Crisman and Robert Allen (Eds.), *Court of Appeal* (New York: Ballantine, 1992); bell hooks, *Ain't I A Woman?* (Boston: South End Press, 1981).

[54]See especially Joanne Carlson Brown and Carole R. Bohn (Eds.), *Christianity, Patriarchy, and Abuse: A Feminist Critique* (New York: Pilgrim Press, 1989).

[55]See, for example, Mary Daly, Rosemary Ruether, and Gerda Lerner, *The Creation of Patriarchy* (New York: Oxford University Press, 1986).

[56]Barbara Ehrenreich, Elizabeth Hess, & Gloria Jacobs, *Remaking Love: The Feminization of Sex* (Garden City, NY: Anchor Books, 1987).

[57]"As a group, white men expose their hatred by increased exploitation of women as sex objects to sell products and by their wholehearted support of pornography and rape. Black men expose their hatred by increased domestic brutality (white men also) and their vehement verbal denouncement of black women as matriarchs, castrators, bitches, etc." *Ain't I A Woman*, p. 102.

[58]See, for example, *The Christian Century*, 1993, Vol. 50, (Jan. 20), p. 50.

[59]Pamela Couture, *Blessed Are the Poor? Women's Poverty, Family Policy and Practical Theology* (Nashville, TN: Abingdon Press, 1991), p. 100, 133.

[60]As an example of what the church is doing, see Robert E. Horton, "Sexual Abuse: What Can We Do?" *Circuit Rider*, 1992 (Sept.), p. 4.

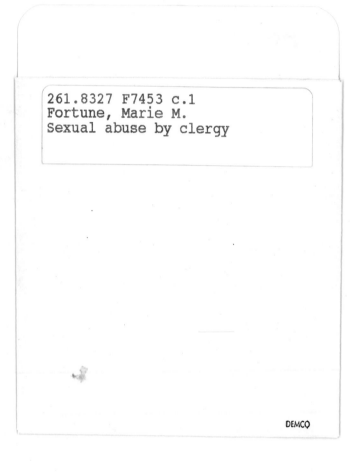